High Fashion in Shakespeare's Time

Andrew Brownfoot

Tarquin Publications

Shakespeare's Time

WILLIAM SHAKESPEARE
(1564-1616)

William Shakespeare is held by many to be the world's greatest dramatist and his lifetime spanned the Elizabethan and Jacobean periods of high fashion. His plays were often performed at Court during Elizabeth's reign and when James came to the throne they became even more popular. Incidentally, the word 'Jacobean' comes from 'Jacobus' the Latin form for James used in most official documents of the time.

James himself became the patron of Shakespeare's company, making them 'The King's Men" and Shakespeare became, in effect, a royal servant. He became a man of standing and position, in spite of the fact that generally theatrical people were considered to be on the fringes of society. Certainly he preferred to be thought of as a gentleman and a poet, and by the end of his life he was indeed just that.

Little is known about Shakespeare's early life but he moved from Stratford upon Avon to London in about 1587 and probably worked initially as an actor in one of the many theatres there. The first recorded public performance of a play written by him was in March 1592 when there was a production called "Harry the Sixth" at the Rose Theatre. This was probably the first of the three parts of Henry VI. It was an immediate success and in the next few years he was to write prolifically and with continuing success.

His plays reflect the structure of the society in which he lived and are often set in royal courts and concern the activities of important people: kings and queens, emperors, princes and nobles. Throughout his life he was to see and comment on the extravagant styles of dress developed by the wealthy elite to gain, demonstrate, and maintain their superiority.

These four pictures give a general impression of how fashionable sihouettes changed during Shakespeare's lifetime.

Around 1560

Around 1580

In Shakespeare's time, clothing and fashion played a part of such importance that we can scarcely comprehend it today. There was an enormous gulf between the aristocratic and wealthy who owned vast estates and the ordinary people who owned very little. This gulf was emphasised and reinforced by the fashions and manners of the day.

Most fashionable people revelled in the fact that an outward display of wealth and success served to emphasise the difference between them, the privileged few, and the poor majority. If you were good-looking, amusing, brilliantly dressed and in the right place at the right time, there was always the chance that you could do very well indeed. Men and women vied with each other in the exaggerations of their style and in their search for the latest fashion. They were willing to submit themselves to extremes of discomfort and to restrictions on their movements, that we today would feel to be intolerable. All with the aim of achieving the proud silhouettes that the latest fashion demanded.

However uncomfortable the fashions might be and however difficult it might be to move freely, they clearly demonstrated that you had servants to help and therefore no need to do manual or menial work yourself. Wearing lavish displays of gold, jewels and costly fabrics was also a way of showing other people how wealthy and influential you were. Of course sometimes this impression would be false as someone might have sold everything they had or might have borrowed from money-lenders simply to buy the clothes and jewellery they were wearing.

"She bears a duke's revenues on her back
And in her heart she scorns our poverty"

King Henry VI, Part II

A well-dressed wife was another opportunity that a man had to be able to show to all how wealthy he was. The more extravagant the better! Unmarried daughters might be dressed in the latest fashions in order to attract a husband who would enhance her family's position in society. Love was rarely a consideration in marriage but detailed haggling over dowries, financial settlements and social position most certainly was.

The top places in society were held by the monarch and the royal family and those closest to the monarch might be able to gain astonishing wealth and power as a result of little more than good fortune or a good line in flattery.

The Crown was the ultimate source of wealth and authority in the country and kings and queens were able to grant honours, mansions, castles and huge estates to any one who served them well or who pleased them.

Another route to wealth and power was to be granted a monopoly on the sale of certain products. This meant being given the right to add a tax, an additional sum to the selling prices of the monopoly products. The extra money raised in this way would be paid directly into their own purses and thus contribute to the cost of costumes such as those described in this book. The monopoly on the sale of salt was one of the most lucrative of these burdens on the poor.

Very many people made use of 'patronage' to climb upwards in society. The patron might be a friend, relative or acquaintance higher up in society who could make the necessary introductions. In return the patron would expect either loyal support in dangerous or difficult times or, more commonly, a gift of money or valuables which would help to maintain their own lifestyles. By whatever means, people had to be able to afford their fashionable clothes. Without them they would be excluded from high society and would be doomed to remain poor and unnoticed for evermore.

"I think he bought his doublet in Italy, his round hose in France, his bonnet in Germany and his behaviour everywhere"

The Merchant Of Venice

Throughout this period, foreign fashions were always in demand. First Italian then German styles, followed by French. Polish and even Flemish. None of these influences were entirely discarded but Spanish style was the one which was most admired and reproduced.

In the fashion guide which follows there is a description in alphabetical order of the main items which contributed to high fashion in Shakespeare's time and the pull-up scenes and the illustrations which surround the diaries show the rich elaboration of style and costume which made it such an interesting period of our history.

Around 1590

Around 1610

Armed

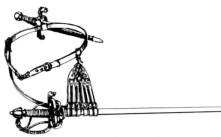

Weapons were carried by all men in what was a violent age, but as with everything else, great distinction was made between the wealthy and the poor. A fashionable man would never be seen in public without being armed with an elaborately designed **rapier** and a dagger worn high on the back of the sword belt. The dagger was principally used to parry blows from an opponent's sword but was also handy for stabbing, cutting an enemy's throat or peeling an apple.

Bands

Band was the general term given to the separate **collars** and cuffs made of linen which from the middle of the century were heavily starched and often edged with newly introduced lace from Italy. Band boxes were provided to store these expensive and delicate items - strangely we now put hats and dresses in them.

Bodies or Pair of Bodies

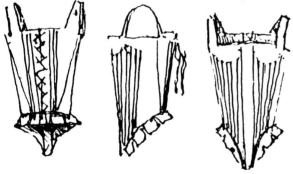

What we would call a corset. At this time they were heavily stiffened with rushes or, later in this period, whale bone. The centre front was strengthened further with an extra strong and long **busk**. Some girls wore such a corset from the age of about five, enabling a very narrow look to be achieved by restricting the growth of the rib-cage.

Bombast

A cotton wadding used to pad out men's **trunk hose** and **doublets** to make them appear more impressive and substantial. The word is now used to describe pompous speech and behaviour.

Bum Roll

A padded or boned roll which exaggerated a woman's hips and the smallness of her waist. The **petticoats** or skirts it held out then fell vertically to the ankle or below for formal occasions. See **Farthingale**.

Busk

A long piece of wood, bone, ivory or metal which held the front of the corset rigidly straight when slipped into the slots provided. Busk laces were then fastened at the end to prevent it being pushed out of place when the wearer bent or sat.

Cape or Cloak

Capes were worn by both sexes, but the short style was particularly a male fashion and almost invariably the most expensive item of a man's outfit. When Sir Walter Raleigh spread his cloak in the mud to save the Queen's embroidered shoes it was an extravagant and effective gesture, calculated to attract her Majesty's attention. The cloak in question was probably worth the value of a house and several hundred acres of good farmland. Portraits show him wearing capes lavishly embroidered in designs entirely made of pearls.

Ceruse

The poisonous mixture containing white lead and vinegar used as a cosmetic by women, and some men, in order to create the admired white, aristocratic complexion that proclaimed the wearer to be above menial outside work.

Chemise or Smock

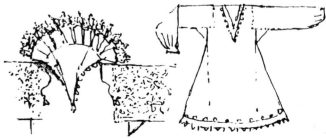

A feminine shirt, often decorated with embroidery or the new lace from Italy. A strange misreading of the law led to many women being married, dressed only in their smock. In doing so , it was believed that she allowed her husband to remain free of all her debts, either existing or in the future.

Codpiece

A pouch for the male private parts made necessary by the extreme high cut of their **hose**. To us a rather indelicate item but at the time it was subject to the exaggerations of fashion.

Collars

Spanish fashions of the 1560s and 1570s imposed rigid, high collars that made turning the head almost impossible but made the wearer look awesomely dignified. When frivolity or impertinence were suspected the wearer could swing the whole torso round, in rebuke, rather than the head alone.

Dagging - see **Piccadilloes**

Diapers

In England we call these nappies, but in America the term is still in common use. Children wore diapers until the age of five, they were not fully weaned or trained until then. Boys wore the same skirts as girls to cover their diapers but wore men's hats and **doublets**.

Doublet

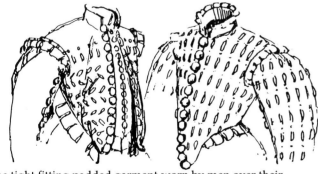

The tight fitting padded garment worn by men over their waistcoats. Lavishly decorated and in 1588 cut and stuffed in the exaggerated, almost feminine, Peascod or Goose belly form. This paunch was so difficult and hot to wear, it was frequently left undone and fastened only when strict formality was necessary.

Dingen van den Passe - see **Starch**

Etiquette

With such difficult clothes and swords to manage, it was very important to learn the art of correct movement and manners. Many people employed dancing masters to teach them how to move and behave in society.

Farthingale

There were two basic types of this skirt-extending device. The original style known as the Spanish Farthingale created a stiff inverted conical shape, with the use of stiffened hoops, usually of wood or rope. The French Farthingale held the skirt out from the top with a padded or boned roll (known as a **Bum Roll** in England) and the skirt then fell vertically to the ankle. Even more extreme styles were achieved by the use of a series of rolls fixed together and extending outwards from the waist or by the use of a wooden or iron hoop, sometimes 4 feet in diameter. This hoop was attached by tightly drawn pleats to the waist and held the skirt higher at the back than at the front.

Galligaskins

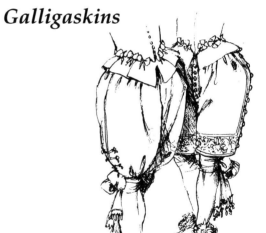

A type of loose fitting breeches, either closed or open at the knee. Originally worn in Gascony (hence the name) they became popular with the introduction of knitted silk stockings. More comfortable than the stylish **trunk hose**, they eventually replaced them.

Gloves

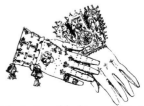

One of the great luxuries of fashion at this time, and as Shakespeare's father found, in his profession as a glove maker, people were prepared to spend large sums of money to buy them. Often made of the finest perfumed leather and then richly embroidered with gold and silver thread, they were one of the most popular gifts to powerful patrons.

Hats, Hoods and Headdresses

Men's hats formed an important part of the rules of etiquette when greetings were exchanged. When the wool trade was flagging, a law was passed commanding that all men below a certain income level must wear a woollen cap (called the 'Statute Cap') to church on Sundays or pay a fine. During Elizabeth's reign soft styles were preferred. They were known as bonnets and they varied hugely in both style and decoration. Later, in the Jacobean period, they were replaced by blocked hats. Most women wore the 'French Hood', a development of a medieval style that continued well into the seventeenth century. Fashionable women at court sometimes wore men's hats to display their comparative emancipation. However on formal occasions various elaborate headdresses were arranged in the hair, with feathers, long wired veils and lavish jewellery.

Hose

Masculine tights, which at times were cut so high that a **codpiece** became necessary.

Knickers or Draws

These were not worn except by the more cultivated ladies of the Italian Court, so falling off a horse could be a considerable source of embarrassment.

Lists

Lists were the unsightly outside or selvage edge of certain woven fabrics such as velvet or brocade that would normally be turned in or cut away. However it became a popular fashion to make up garments out of decorative strips of such materials.

Married Head

After marriage women wore their hair up and frequently covered. Queen Elizabeth ostentatiously wore her hair falling on her shoulders as "The Virgin Queen".

Mistress

Mistress was the proper title for a married woman at this time. For example Mistress Ford in "The Merry Wives of Windsor". We now only use the abbreviated form Mrs.

Panes

Strips of material arranged vertically as a decorative feature, usually seen on sleeves or **trunk hose.**

Pantobles or Pantoufles

What we would call slippers or mules. They were frequently made for use as overshoes to protect high fashion shoes which were often pale and elaborately decorated. Pantobles were difficult to manage and they easily came off.

Petticoat

To the Elizabethans this word described any skirt that was not permanently fixed to the bodice. In winter many petticoats were worn, one on top of another, for warmth. Scarlet seems to have been a popular colour. Mary, Queen of Scots chose a crimson petticoat for her execution in 1587, so that her blood would not spoil the effect of her ensemble.

Piccadilloes or Dagging

The fashion, introduced from Spain, of scalloped or slashed edging, was usually seen at the waist, neck or shoulder. Often used to mask eyelet holes through which laces were passed to fasten sleeves, skirt or **trunk hose** to the **body.** Some people claim that Piccadilly is named in memory of a tailor's shop which first introduced the fashion to London.

Rapier

The fashionable sword of a gentleman which needed skill to manage, even for the simple act of sitting down. Its long narrow blade, although covered by a scabbard, had to be tucked closely to the outstretched left leg where it could be more easily seen. Otherwise someone might trip over it and challenge you to a duel. Causing anyone to lose his dignity could be very dangerous and might be fatal!

Ruffs

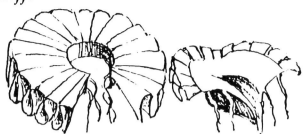

Originally a ruff was any form of decoration made of gathered material. We now think of ruffs as the elaborately pleated and starched collars of the Shakespearean age. They were formed by pleating and fixing strips of material, either straight or curved, to a band. They were almost impossible to maintain and so became highly valued as a display of wealth.

Shirt

Usually made of linen, this male undergarment was generously cut and on occasion elaborately decorated with cut and drawn thread work that could be displayed when the **doublet** was undone. The neck was fastened with band strings or tiny buttons and gathered into a little frill. Later this frill developed into the separate elaboration known as a **ruff**.

Shoes

At the beginning of the period we are looking at, shoes were narrow and tight fitting with no heel. For the fashionable, the uppers were made of fine leather and decorated with embroidery and arrangements of little slashes and punched holes. Towards the end of Elizabeth's life, shoes developed a slight wedge at the heel which became a definite and quite high heel by the 1600s. Little difference was made between the styles for men or women and, more often than not, the shoes were made to be worn on either foot.

Sitting

The late Elizabethans when fashionably dressed, their limbs and bodies stiffened by boned and padded styles, found the simple act of sitting difficult and arduous. Most people had to stand when in the royal presence, but if invited to sit they usually propped themselves on the edge of a highly cushioned stool. Armchairs were only for the host or most privileged guests and chairs with backs were an early seventeenth century invention. When out of doors, men reclined on their bombasted stomachs in the 'Roman' manner.

Starch

Used to stiffen **ruffs** and **bands**, the recipes were highly guarded trade secrets. Frau Dingen van den Passe, who starched and set the royal ruffs, was able to charge four times the daily pay of the Admiral of the Fleet for lessons in her skills. A fashion for coloured starches took hold in the first years of James's reign, mainly because in Spain only the royal princesses were allowed to wear coloured ruffs. A Mrs. Turner invented the yellow starch, so hated by King James, which none the less remained high fashion until she was publicly hanged wearing one of her own creations. She, allegedly, murdered Sir Thomas Overbury in the Tower.

Stockings

Hand knitted silk stockings were first popular in Spain and were introduced to England early in the sixteenth century. However it was not until an English clergyman, William Lee, invented his stocking frame that they became widely available. He presented the first pair to Queen Elizabeth in 1589, after which she refused to wear anything else. Men also wore them at the end of her reign, and they eventually replaced the tight **hose** that had been the fashion for over a hundred years.

Stomacher

A triangular piece of fabric usually highly decorated. Placed over and masking the centre front fastening of the corset or doublet.

Smock - see Chemise

Strossers

Men's underpants; they were cut on the cross for tight fitting, with a pouch in front and they were made with many different leg lengths from none at all to those reaching to the ankle.

Trunk Hose

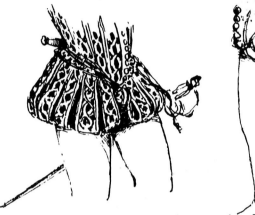

The padded covering of men's upper thighs. They were of many shapes and sizes but in 1588 the most typical was the extremely short variety that from the back view left much of the buttocks covered only by the high cut hose. They were usually decorated with strips of fabric, known as **panes**, matching the **doublet**.

Trussing

Tight lacing was an essential part of dressing to achieve the fashionable silhouettes of both sexes. **Bodies, doublet** and **hose** all had to be stretched to the limit at all times to avoid unsightly wrinkles. When men engaged in strenuous activities or sat on low seats it was necessary to undo some or all the fastenings that held up the hose. When Hamlet was seen by Ophelia with his hose "down gyved" it was taken by her to be a sure sign of madness.

Under-propper

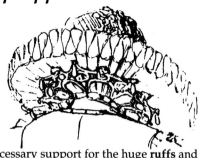

The very necessary support for the huge **ruffs** and **collars** now fashionable. They were either of stiffened linen, or wire constructions, more or less elaborate according to taste and pocket.

Veil

Made of delicate, translucent, light materials, veils were very popular for women's head wear. Queen Elizabeth was particularly fond of them and by the 1580s she commonly wore veils wired out into great curving wing-like structures. The wires were usually fixed from the **headdress** and then attached to the shoulders and from that point the veil hung unwired to form a train at the back of her gown. With this style, whenever the Queen moved her head there was always the danger that her wig would remain facing forward, whatever her head might do!

Waistcoat

A tight fitting undergarment of linen, sometimes quilted and covered with more expensive fabric. It was usually dropped over the head on top of the **smock** or shirt and tight laced at the sides or back. The woman's **petticoat** and skirt or the man's **hose** were held up by being laced to the waist of this garment.

Whisk

The flat, stiffly starched and supported collar made familiar to us by the famous 'portrait' published with the First Folio of Shakespeare's plays. It was especially popular in Spain and continued to be worn there long after the rest of Europe had discarded the fashion.

The Daily Journals
&
Pull-up Scenes
1588 and 1606

Let us now meet the three diarists and through their journals,
glimpse fashionable life in Court circles at this time in history.
The writers are imaginary and their journals are invented but
they comment on the events of the time and their concern
for fashion mirrors that of the real people they meet.

Lord Thomas Conhem   **Lady Alice Conhem**   **Lord Henry Goodworth**

On May 8th 1588 Alice, the daughter of Sir John and Lady Jane Neworth marries Lord Thomas Conhem, a match which will considerably raise her position in society. She is nineteen, and in her diary written on her wedding day, she tells how she dressed for the service and for the splendid feast afterwards. She also explains why her new husband is not able to be at the feast.

On that same day we can also read the diary of her husband, giving his views of the ceremony and the marriage he has just embarked on. After the ceremony he returns to his lodgings to change his clothes before going to Court for his appointment with Lord Burghley. He is helped to dress by Mistress Bondin, with embarrassing results.

We then move on some 18 years to July 1606 and to meet the third diarist Lord Henry Goodworth. He tells us of his visit to the Tower of London on an errand for the Queen. He feels nervous about going there and appears from his journals to be a rather unfortunate man with a special affinity for water!

The Court is to entertain the King of Denmark at Theobolds, the magnificent new home of Robert Cecil, and there is to be hunting during the day and a Masque Ball late into the evening. Both Lord Henry and Lady Alice have been invited.

Alice's husband Thomas had been executed some four years earlier for his part in the plot by the Earl of Essex to bring down the government, but Alice herself had remained on friendly terms with Robert Cecil. Hence the invitation and the coach which was sent to fetch her. What should she wear to such a glittering occasion?

Lord Henry's position at Court meant that he was obliged to go hunting with the King, in spite of being an unenthusiastic horseman. Perhaps it is with good reason that he is always worrying about the state of his expensive clothes!

And what did happen on that disastrous evening at Theobolds when a plate of jelly is tipped into the lap of the King of Denmark?

All the world's a stage...

...And all the men and women in it merely players.
They have their exits and their entrances;
And one man in his time plays many parts.

QUEEN ELIZABETH I
(1533-1603)

One of England's most popular monarchs, cunning, calculating, flirtatious with her favourites and fortunate in her advisors. She reigned for 45 years. Her flirtations with Raleigh and Essex, while lucrative for them, were only pleasant diversions from the real passion of her life, the exercise of royal power and government.

KING JAMES VI & I
(1566-1624)

The abdication of his mother, Mary Queen of Scots, made him King James VI of Scotland when he was only six months old and when Queen Elizabeth died in 1603 he was also next in line for the English throne. James therefore became the first King of the United Kingdom. Never the most dignified of men, he couldn't resist shouting abuse at ladies, who were watching his coronation procession from their first floor windows. He disliked their new-fashioned yellow starched ruffs. Several plots against his life left him nervous and distrustful and an unkind critic reported that he was slovenly in his habits and spoke in a strong Scots accent with a tongue that was too big for his mouth. James had a passion for hunting and meddling in religious affairs and a weakness for drink.

A Chronology of Events

1558
Queen Elizabeth came to the throne

1564
The birth of William Shakespeare

1566
King James born, son of Mary, Queen of Scots

1587
Mary Queen of Scots executed at Fotheringay Castle
William Shakespeare arrived in London.

1588
The defeat of the Spanish Armada

Part I of the journals

1590
Anne of Denmark married James VI of Scotland

1592
First performance of a Shakespeare play

1601
Essex executed

1603
Death of Elizabeth I, James VI became James I of England
The Main and Bye Plots

1605
The Gunpowder Plot

1606
King Christian of Denmark's visit

Part II of the journals

1616
Death of William Shakespeare

William Cecil
(1521-1598)

Robert Cecil
(1563-1612)

Queen Anne
(1576-1619)

Walter Raleigh
(c.1552-1618)

King Christian
(1577-1648)

William Cecil, First Baron Burghley

For forty years he was Secretary of State and in effect chief minister to Queen Elizabeth. His cool logic and skill at changing direction to avoid disaster or gain advantage was to earn him the nickname "The Fox". This was given by envious people who failed to appreciate his truly honest and hard working character. Without him and Robert, his second son, the Elizabethan age could not have been so glorious.

Robert Cecil, First Earl of Salisbury

The crippled younger son of William Cecil. Charming and discreet in manner, he had a brilliant political career in both Elizabeth's and James's reigns. He was created Lord Salisbury in 1605 and became, like his father, Secretary of State and Chief Minister to the Crown. King James called Robert "My wee mon". Robert's wife Elizabeth, died in 1597. It is likely that when King James's Court visited him at **Theobalds** in July 1606 his three surviving children **William**, **Frances** and **Catherine** were there to help entertain the visitors. Catherine was then ten years old and like her father slightly deformed. At that time deformities were considered by most people as a sign of devilish influence or at best an affliction to be laughed at.

Queen Anne, Princess of Denmark

She married King James in 1590. Anne was a good natured but not very bright woman, who loved childish games. Many a lady's court dress was ruined in order to satisfy Her Majesty's pleasure in games such as 'Rise Pig and Go' and 'Fire!'. In a court full of intrigue and malice, the Queen, for all her faults, remained kind and honest.

Sir Walter Raleigh

Adventurer, courtier and poet, he was a favourite of Queen Elizabeth but later he unwittingly became involved in the **Bye** plot. Many of his associates were involved, and implicated him and he was sentenced to be hung, drawn and quartered. His execution was deferred and he remained a prisoner in The Tower of London for many years. In the spring of 1606 he suffered a stroke but by July he had recovered enough to distil medicines in the laboratory which he had set up in his quarters. His Balsam of Guiana was especially popular with Queen Anne. Thanks to his wife, Lady Elizabeth, Sir Walter lived in considerable style in the Tower in spite of the efforts of **Sir William Wadd** to curb it by imposing as many petty regulations as he could. He was given one last opportunity to bring wealth from the new world but the adventure failed and he was beheaded in 1618.

Christian IV, King of Denmark

Christian had grandiose ideas that he and and his kingdom could lead the Protestant cause to victory against the Catholic League. His visit to England in 1606 was not just to visit his sister but was also an attempt to persuade King James to join the fight. James's instinct, encouraged by Robert Cecil, was to make peace with Spain so he would do nothing to help. Christian wanted Sir Walter Raleigh to become Admiral of the Danish Fleet but James refused to release him. The Court entertained King Christian in style while he was in England but moved away from London to avoid the plague. At Greenwich the festivities were enlivened with a performance of "Hamlet, Prince of Denmark".

Plots and Treason

Queen Elizabeth always refused to name a successor, and it was only the manoeuvrings of the astute Robert Cecil which made it possible for James to mount the English throne without serious opposition. However there were several plots against the king, in particular the **Main** and **Bye** plots. These attempts to overthrow the king were ill-organised and were soon detected by the agents of Robert Cecil. Many other powerful people also employed spies or agents, hoping to gain an advantage of some kind

One source of grievance was that James had promised to ease the restrictions placed apon Roman Catholics but this in turn made the Puritans angry. All the old hatreds which were simmering out of sight while the Queen lived, came to the surface and James nervously withdrew the promises to the Catholics.

In 1605 a group of Catholics, including Guy Fawkes, was discovered in the act of attempting to blow up the Houses of Parliament with the King and Government inside. As he had done before, Robert Cecil watched and waited until the very last moment in order to make the discovery more dramatic. He was therefore able to increase the hatred of the king's enemies felt by the public.

The hanging, drawing and quartering of the conspirators was watched by an eager crowd in holiday mood and we still celebrate their deaths today!

Lady Alice Conhem's Journal May 4th 1588

Today is my marriage day and I am not to dress until after the ceremony. Mother is upset at this arrangement and I am disappointed. Father says we should not be so foolish. It is but a small thing to please my lord who has so honoured me with marriage. I am to wear my gown at the great feast following the service and so everyone will see what splendid state we keep.

It is now late and I await my Lord. My chemise was so much easier to kneel in than my marriage gown would have been. How clever of My Lord Thomas to think of this.

After the ceremony I ran back to my chambers to dress. Everything was prepared and laid out ready. Martha and Mary held out my waistcoat as I ran through the door and dropped it over my head, saying "Now you are in the trap madam!" They joked in this way all the while as they laced my waistcoat and petticoat together. My hair took so much time to dress and curl and I am sure my neck will never feel warm again. Now I have a married head.

When I told Martha that my Lord had had to return to court on business and would miss his own wedding feast, she was so surprised that she burnt her finger on the curling tongs! But I reassured her that he had promised to return as soon as he could. Mary was obliged to re-paint my face, the first time she had done this alone. She was so nervous that she dropped the ceruse, narrowly missing my petticoat. Oh what a mess, but at last I was ready to robe. Martha had great difficulty lacing my bodies and tying in the busk. Her poor finger started to bleed and a bandage had to be found, to save my dress from damage.

The size of my farthingale drew cries of admiration from the girls and alarmed me, not a little. I tried the door and found I could get through! I have never worn the French style before and find it quite easy to wear, allowing so much freedom for the legs. Pinning the stomacher to my bodies caused some pain for Martha and so Mary took over the task, pinning the over gown and tying my sleeves under the piccadilloes at the shoulder.

With my ruffs in place, all that remained was the beautiful veil, wired in the same way as her Majesty's. Poor Martha was determined, in spite of her finger, to fix this last extravagance, a present from my Lord's mother. It took a little longer than I had hoped but I bore it with patience for her sake.

The guests were much impressed as I stood to receive them. But my greatest triumph was still to come, in spite of My Lord Thomas's absence from the feast. We deserted the Great High Chamber, while the tables were removed for the dancing. Dear Michael Hicks contrived to introduce me to Mr. Cecil, Lord Burghley's son. Mr. Cecil has such a sensitive face and such intelligent conversation, that his deformity is instantly forgot. We sat, both with great circumspection because of our French style, and talked until the fanfare called us to return from the Banqueting House to dance.

This diagram shows how the thread links the four pieces so that they will pull up together and make a three-dimensional scene.

Start with the backmost piece and sew through the pairs of points. Go through them several times so that the thread does not slip. They are marked ● ●

Allow enough thread between the pieces so that it is taut when the figures lie flat.

Glue the pull tag to a short piece of thread at the front.

PULL TAG

The Wedding Feast
The Wedding Feast

A
B C
D

Score along the dotted lines and cut out these pieces while looking at this side of the paper.

Cut along the blue ouline. Do not cut any closer to the figures.

Glue the pieces to page 15 in alphabetical order and then link them with thread as shown in the diagram.

Guests

Lady Jane Neworth

Musician

Sir John Neworth and Lady Conhem

CUT ALONG THIS LINE

E   E

A

B

D

C

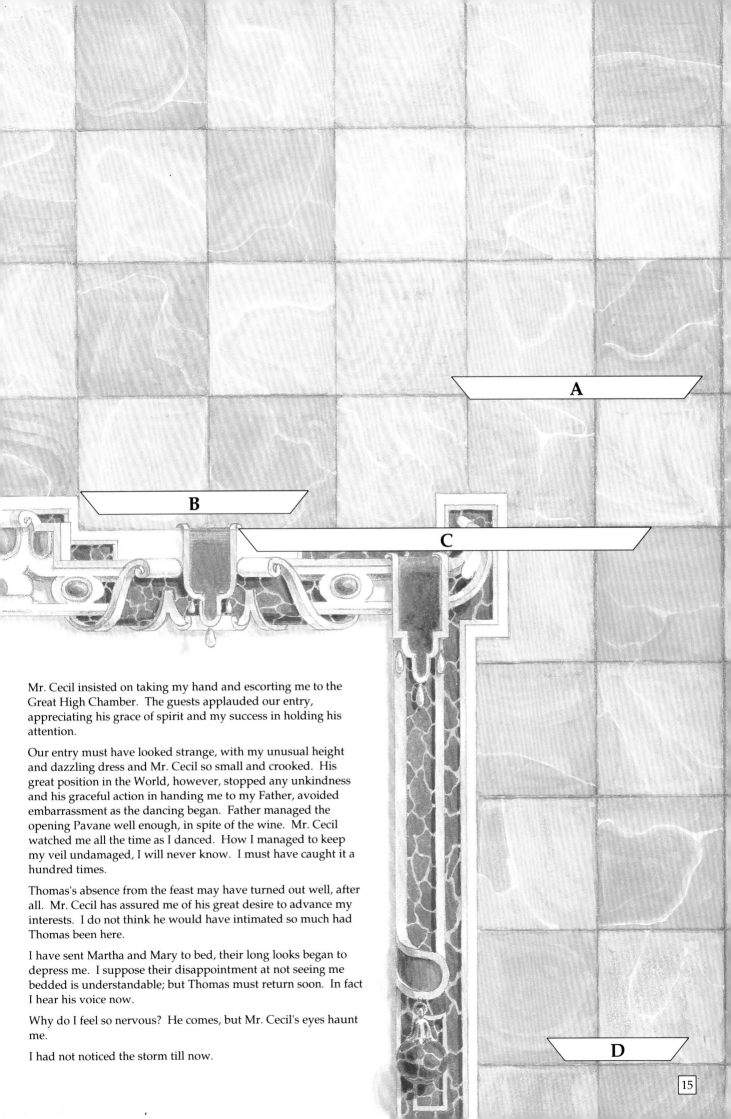

A

B

C

Mr. Cecil insisted on taking my hand and escorting me to the Great High Chamber. The guests applauded our entry, appreciating his grace of spirit and my success in holding his attention.

Our entry must have looked strange, with my unusual height and dazzling dress and Mr. Cecil so small and crooked. His great position in the World, however, stopped any unkindness and his graceful action in handing me to my Father, avoided embarrassment as the dancing began. Father managed the opening Pavane well enough, in spite of the wine. Mr. Cecil watched me all the time as I danced. How I managed to keep my veil undamaged, I will never know. I must have caught it a hundred times.

Thomas's absence from the feast may have turned out well, after all. Mr. Cecil has assured me of his great desire to advance my interests. I do not think he would have intimated so much had Thomas been here.

I have sent Martha and Mary to bed, their long looks began to depress me. I suppose their disappointment at not seeing me bedded is understandable; but Thomas must return soon. In fact I hear his voice now.

Why do I feel so nervous? He comes, but Mr. Cecil's eyes haunt me.

I had not noticed the storm till now.

D

Lord Thomas Conhem's Journal May 4th 1588

I am well pleased with today's arrangements. My feigned ill humour soon persuaded Sir John to agree to my demands. Lord, how eager some people are to rise in the world! Fortunately he seems ignorant of the reason for my insistence on a smocked bride and Alice, foolishly, believes it to be my romantic passion. Now the ceremony is done I shall get a substantial income from her estates and, thanks to her simple attire, I remain free of her debts.

Sir John and Lady Jane witnessed the ceremony looking like two stuffed capons, no doubt trying to give some dignity to the occasion. Alice put me in mind of the burgers of Calais, so nervous and fragile in her smock and I, still booted, spurred and armed, obviously put the fear of God into the ignorant preacher. The ceremony over, I fled from the horrid country life of Hammersmith, back to the City, pretending urgent business at Court.

Mistress Bondin was at my lodgings when I arrived and helped me out of my clothes and bad temper, but was put out when I said I must dress for Court immediately. "I see", she said,"You have a prick of conscience". I ignored her and struggled into my strossers without her help. Bondin had been to Frau Dingen van den Passe to collect my new ruff. Frau Dingen is truly a genius, but since the Queen has used her, she costs a royal fortune.

My shirt on, Tom brought hot water to shave me and put the curling tongs in the fire to heat. Once shaved, Tom went to collect the curlers. I had to remind the fool that waistcoats have to be dropped over the head, and I had not yet donned mine. Mistress Bondin was determined to help in trussing me and managed to snap two of the laces of my trunk hose.

Tom went in search of replacements, leaving me at the mercy of Bondin. He returned to find me flushed and complaining that the trussing was too severe. His reply was simple, did I want to impress My Lord Burghley or Mistress Bondin? Biting my lips I said nothing, but sat with slow dignity, for my hair to be curled.

Tom was suddenly still and quiet, it was the smell of burning hair that explained all. Bondin collapsed with laughter at which Tom rushed at her, swearing he would brand her for what she was. Her exit was timely and Tom's use of the curling tongs had restored my humour, and cooled them enough to continue my hair.

Hosed and gartered, Tom helped me into my new doublet; the best peascod I have seen, and the goldsmith's work on the buttons has never been equalled. Tom and I were in a fret over the precious ruff, it seemed impossible to adjust over the under-propper without damage. At last it was fastened and Tom buttoned my doublet, I am quite unable to see my body beneath, only the tight lacing lets me know it's still there. I was maddened to find the hood of my Spanish cape was too small to accommodate the great size of my ruff. Damn the rogue who persuaded me to mix Spanish and French style! But there was nothing to be done, if I wished to make any impression at court.

With my rapier and dagger fastened in position, Tom helped me into my pantobles. He then handed me my gloves, a present from Alice. The fingers seem a little large, but the gold lace trim make them too impressive to be abandoned.

I was half way down the Strand, when the winds caught my ruff. My head was nearly off before I reached shelter. The Gods then had more in store, some jade opened a window above and, without warning, emptied her night soil, stinking at my feet. I leapt back and so avoided the worst but in so doing, my right pantoble came off and I put my unprotected shoe into the mud. There was no point in trying to retrieving the filthy overshoe, so I abandoned the other and hurried off, cursing, to My Lord Burghley.

My hurrying, of course, was a mistake as I caught my trunk hose on a nail and ripped one of the panes away at the top. I managed to hook it up again and held it in place, throughout the entire interview with Lord Burghley. He received me with more affability than I had hoped for. I had no idea that Sir John and Lady Jane were held in such esteem at court. My Lord seemed amused that I should be with him in London, when his son was a guest at my wedding feast in Hammersmith! How was it that I was not told?

My business done, I returned to my lodgings. As I did so the heavens opened and ruined my ruff. My arrival caused much mirth, with my ruff flopped like a rag around my shoulders and starch, running in rivulets, staining my doublet. A curse on Frau Dingen!

I shall enjoy a pipe of tobacco before returning to that appalling house in Hammersmith.

Lord Henry Goodworth's Journal July 7th, 1606

I slept but little and in my shirt and strossers, filled with dread on this morning's mission. Perhaps the phantoms in my mind were summoned by last night's entertainment; a new play by Mr. Shakespeare - witches, murders and revengeful spirits. I wonder their Majesties were so taken, it being so close to the King's experience and set in Scotland.

Why have I been sent on this mission? Was I not cleared of all suspicion in the Bye plot? My severest Spanish style will give stern dignity and also disguise my fearful progress.

Zounds what fools do phantoms make of men! So much fright over four bottles of cordial!

I was rowed down river to the Tower from Hampton Court, the weather overcast and the waters disturbed. As we approached London Bridge distant thunder made me look up to see traitors heads, impaled, looking down. A splash at my side proved to be a jaw dropped from one of these, some beard remained and one that I knew. This were impossible unless by some malicious handiwork. Shaken, I watched it sink as we glid past. I think I managed to hide my fear. I was almost relieved to reach the Tower! The unnatural silence of the plagued City was palpable.

As I stepped off the barge Sir William Waad himself came to greet me. His manner was cold and I thought resentful but he took me to Sir Walter and left us alone. Raleigh has aged and I was sad to see him so low. Three years a prisoner and under threat of death, would have killed a lesser man. He assures me that though his speech is somewhat slurred, he is much improved and the movement in his left hand is almost back to normal.

Score along the dotted lines and cut out these pieces while looking at this side of the paper.

Cut along the grey ouline. Do not cut any closer to the figures.

Glue the pieces to page 21 in alphabetical order and then link them with thread as shown in the diagram.

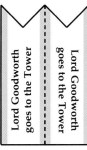

Lord Goodworth goes to the Tower

Lord Goodworth goes to the Tower

PULL TAG

This diagram shows how the thread links the three pieces so that they will pull up together and make a three-dimensional scene.

Start with the backmost piece and sew through the pairs of points. Go through them several times so that the thread does not slip. They are marked ● ●

Allow enough thread between the pieces so that it is taut when the figures lie flat.

Glue the pull tag to a short piece of thread at the front.

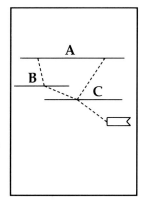

Lord Henry Goodworth

A spy

The hired boat

CUT ALONG THIS LINE

19

B

D
D

C

A

A

B

C

G

He showed me round his experiments and explained the properties of his Balsam of Guiana. Apparently Her Majesty makes use of it and even sometimes comes herself to obtain it, but against the King's wishes. That is why I was there! To bring back four bottles! She often seeks advice from Sir Walter and I think he expects much from her interest. He keeps considerable style, through the persistence of Lady Raleigh, though Sir Walter told me that William Waad has put a curb on her going in and out from the Tower in their magnificent coach.

I was grateful to be returned unnoticed to Hampton and managed to gain my lodgings without seeing anyone of rank. As I was about to step off the barge, its sudden unexpected motion caused me to fall back into the water on the floor at the bargemen's feet. I had not thought before, how absorbent bombast is. As I struggled up again I was horrified to find water cascading from my trunk hose, like from an overfull sponge. Dignity was not possible so a low joke to the oarsmen and a dash to the nearest door was all I could manage.

When I presented myself to Her Majesty, having changed, of course, she quipped that she had heard that I must have been visited by a mermaid! Did she mean my friends at the Mermaid Tavern?
Or had someone witnessed my undignified return? Much profit may it do them.

But she thanked me greatly for the cordial.

Lady Alice Conhem's Journal
July 7th, 1606

Putting on my smock this morning I was reminded of my wedding day eighteen years ago. So much unhappiness since then; but at nineteen I was so easily swayed.

Thomas so headstrong and ambitious...

I thank God dear Lord Salisbury kept his word, but for him I would be....

Enough! Thomas is dead these four years for his part in the Essex affair and I must look to myself.

The plague makes London unsafe and brings more horror round me. My journey to Theobalds is an unexpected relief; Lord Robert is to make a coach at my disposal.

I have not seen him since he was made Earl of Salisbury last year, what with the Powder Treason ...

Oh! Why do I keep dwelling on torture and horror...

What will he think of me? I have aged, and the colour of my hair...

I hope my choice of a Spanish Gown and Farthingale is suitable. I have not ridden in such a coach before...

Certainly the French style would be mistaken....

I thought I heard the coach had arrived but it was the Dead wagon. The men are supposed to call out but the barking of dogs confused their frightful message.

Mary has rescued me from disaster by reminding me that the King dislikes coloured bands and so they have not packed them. I could not bear to be shouted at, as I was at the Coronation.

I pray his Majesty has forgotten my appearance then in a yellow ruff.

The packing is done, but my Bum Rolls are displayed on top!

The coach has arrived and the baggage cannot be rearranged. Martha is to look to my house while I am away. May God protect her.

I had forgot how prodigious Theobalds is, but my welcome removed any nervousness. It is nine years since Lady Elizabeth died and Robert seems to have overcome his sadness.

He sent the children with an escort to greet me at the commencement of the estate. William with his little bride beside him looks so devoted, at 15 he is already a man of the world. Frances as sweet as ever but wearing an immodest hoop. Can it be four years since she was wed? Little Catherine, of course, did not ride out but came to greet me at the door. She moves well considering her infirmities. How cruel Nature can be; she couldn't wait to tell me that she was to be present at the masque and how splendid William would look.

Lord Salisbury rose and met me at the door of the High Great Chamber and prevented me from making the obeisance due to him. My standing in society will be much improved by this token-almost as much as my aching bones were relieved when the journey was complete! My Spanish Farthingale has punished me for my pride, I should have worn a bum roll. My legs are quite bruised by the hoops. All those cushions were quite unable to prevent my being thrown against them. People would think I had been brawling.

Mary is already asleep on her pallet. I have let her sleep inside the door as she seemed alarmed by the strange surroundings. I am kept awake by the bustle of this great house. The Royal Households arrive tomorrow. Mary snores!

Lord Henry   Goodworth's Journal   July 8th, 1606

The Court leaves for My Lord Salisbury's house today and I am to travel in the King's party. I had hoped for the quieter duties, travelling with the baggage. This honour, though much looked for, is heavy on my purse and I, like My Lord Robert, find no pleasure in the chase - though I must say I have a better seat than His Majesty.

Hunting with King James

CUT ALONG THIS LINE

This diagram shows how the thread links the four pieces so that they will pull up together and make a three-dimensional scene.

Start with the backmost piece and sew through the pairs of points. Go through them several times so that the thread does not slip. They are marked ● ●

Allow enough thread between the pieces so that it is taut when the figures lie flat.

Glue the pull tag to a short piece of thread at the front.

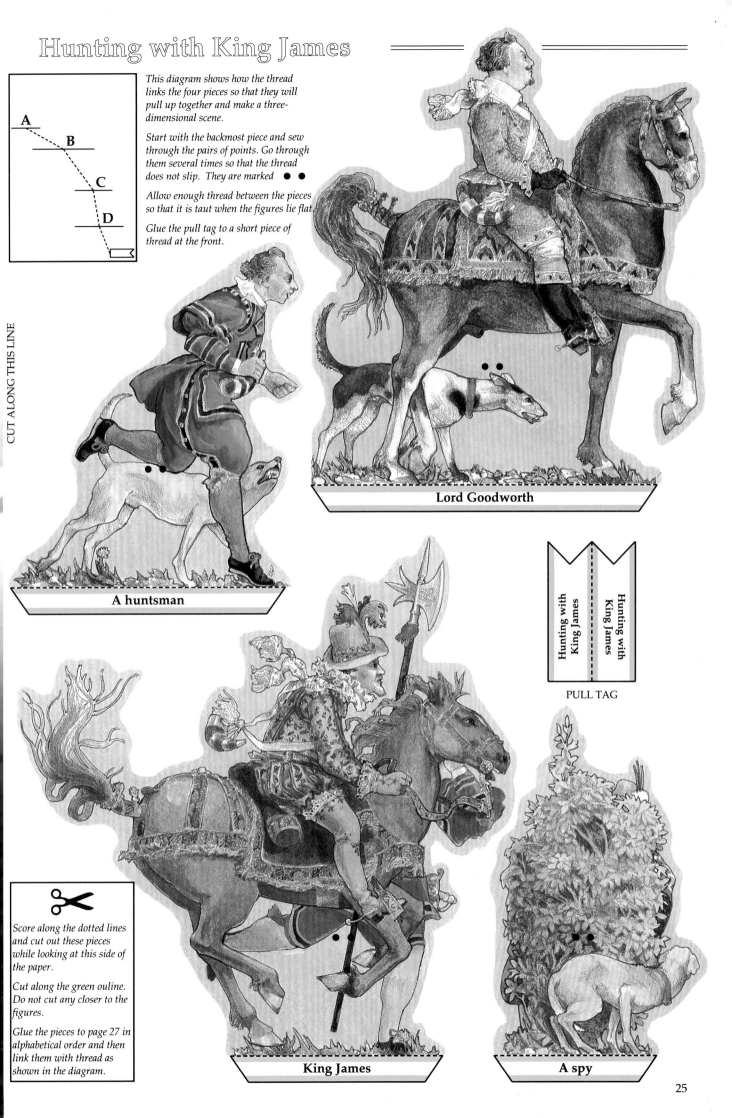

Lord Goodworth

A huntsman

Hunting with King James | Hunting with King James

PULL TAG

Score along the dotted lines and cut out these pieces while looking at this side of the paper.

Cut along the green ouline. Do not cut any closer to the figures.

Glue the pieces to page 27 in alphabetical order and then link them with thread as shown in the diagram.

King James

A spy

B

D

E E

A

C

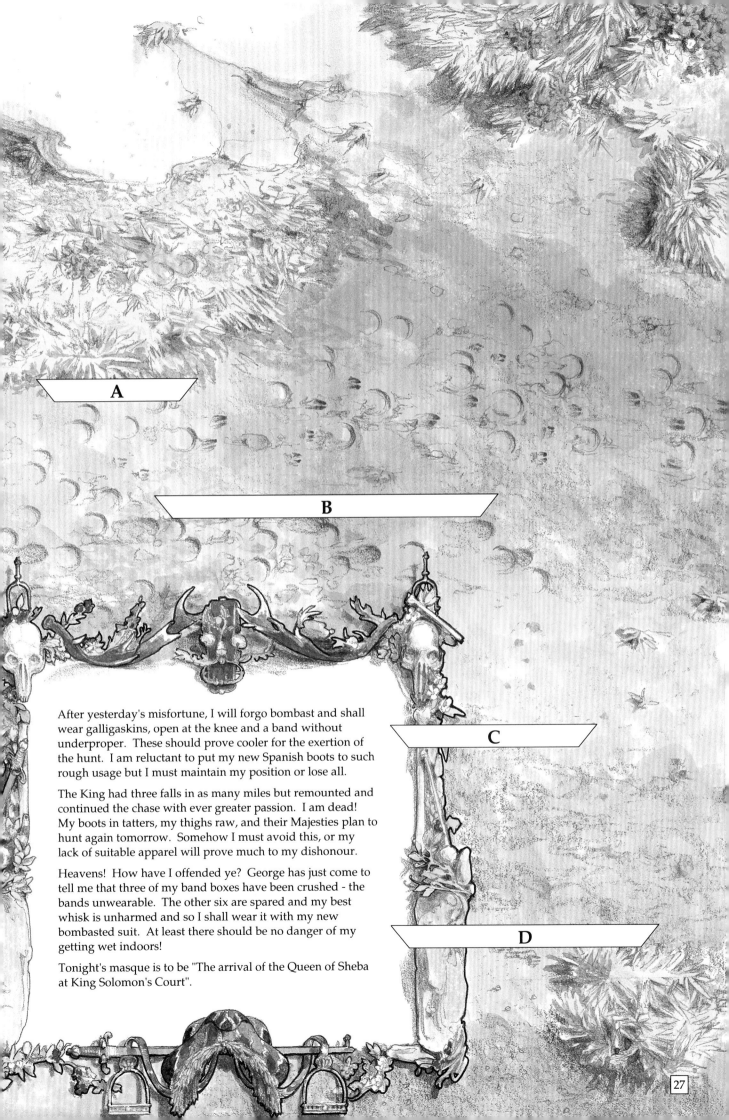

A

B

C

After yesterday's misfortune, I will forgo bombast and shall wear galligaskins, open at the knee and a band without underproper. These should prove cooler for the exertion of the hunt. I am reluctant to put my new Spanish boots to such rough usage but I must maintain my position or lose all.

The King had three falls in as many miles but remounted and continued the chase with ever greater passion. I am dead! My boots in tatters, my thighs raw, and their Majesties plan to hunt again tomorrow. Somehow I must avoid this, or my lack of suitable apparel will prove much to my dishonour.

Heavens! How have I offended ye? George has just come to tell me that three of my band boxes have been crushed - the bands unwearable. The other six are spared and my best whisk is unharmed and so I shall wear it with my new bombasted suit. At least there should be no danger of my getting wet indoors!

Tonight's masque is to be "The arrival of the Queen of Sheba at King Solomon's Court".

D

Lady Alice Conhem's Journal   July 8th, 1606

The day began well. Little Catherine brought up some strawberries and we sat watching the preparations for the hunt. I assured her I would stay with her. I was glad of an excuse to remain in my jacket and petticoat - still feeling stiff and bruised from travelling. We sat for some time until the party rode off. Catherine is such a bright little thing but Robert thinks it unlikely she will ever wed. I am afraid he is all too aware of the cruelties of this world. Catherine is already anxious. She came to me again as I prepared for the entertainment, and asked "Why am I still unwedded? Both William and Frances were married at nine and I am ten. Is that not too old?" I said nothing about my later marriage. After much deliberation and Catherine's admiration, I decided to wear my new wheel farthingale. Then the laces on my under bodies broke - why does this always happen on these occasions? Mary, of course, had several in reserve but Catherine had been playing with them and it took us some time to unravel the knots. She said Sir Walter had taught her some sailor's tricks.

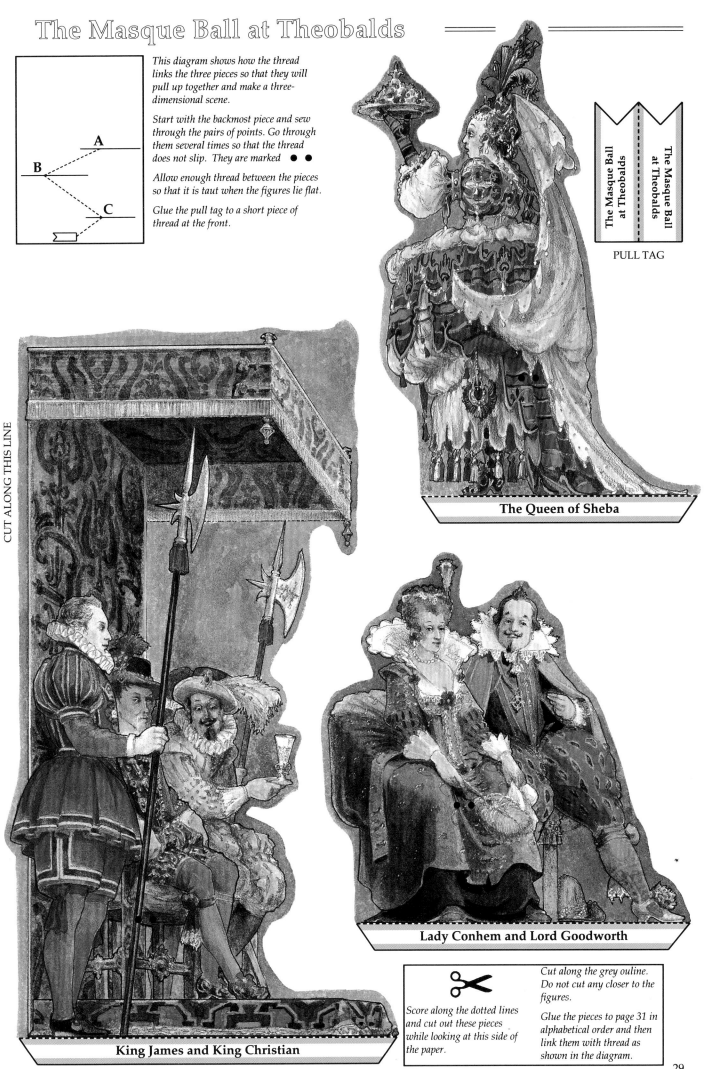

This diagram shows how the thread links the three pieces so that they will pull up together and make a three-dimensional scene.

Start with the backmost piece and sew through the pairs of points. Go through them several times so that the thread does not slip. They are marked ● ●

Allow enough thread between the pieces so that it is taut when the figures lie flat.

Glue the pull tag to a short piece of thread at the front.

A
B
C

PULL TAG

The Masque Ball at Theobalds

The Masque Ball at Theobalds

CUT ALONG THIS LINE

The Queen of Sheba

King James and King Christian

Lady Conhem and Lord Goodworth

Score along the dotted lines and cut out these pieces while looking at this side of the paper.

Cut along the grey ouline. Do not cut any closer to the figures.

Glue the pieces to page 31 in alphabetical order and then link them with thread as shown in the diagram.

29

Once I was laced in and my hair dressed, we started to add my jewellery. When nearly everything had been hung or pinned in place I exclaimed joking "I need to catch a husband". It was all I could do to stop Catherine from rushing to tell her father I needed to wear poor Lady Elizabeth's jewels. Imagine!

I was sat next the widowed Lord Goodworth at the feast. I think Robert has plans for me. Lord Goodworth is somewhat heavy in appearance but his manner is full of wit and his dress, though somewhat over bombastic yet speaks of great wealth and position. I have quite given up the idea of seeking a position at court. Things have sadly changed since our great Queen died. Manners are become deplorable. Robert's great entertainment was made ridiculous and but for the good nature of the King of Denmark, could have brought disaster to the House of Cecil. I must describe the scene, not that I will forget it.

The masque was to represent the Queen of Sheba's visit to Solomon. The scenery was beautiful and the music would have been so, but for the fact that the musicians were drunk. The Queen of Sheba was to present His Majesty of Denmark with sweet refreshment, but being unsteady through wine, fell up the dais and threw jellies, cream and all into His Majesty's lap. I thank Heaven he was amused and not angry, his suit beyond repair. Hurriedly cleaned up, he rose to dance with this silly Queen of Sheba but, being in his cups, he fell and pulled her down with him. King James watched, fidgeting, alone. I am ashamed to say, I was unable to restrain my mirth when 'Faith', 'Hope' and 'Charity' tumbled in, unable to control their movements or speak their lines; and when 'Victory' fell to the ground and just went to sleep, I was helpless with laughter. Matters did not improve when 'Peace' stormed in, lambasting everyone in reach with her olive branch. Our courtiers behave far worse than common players and look as vulgar.

However I must admit that my spirits are much roused by this folly and hope some advantage will come from Lord Goodworth's interest. He, poor man, came to me this morning with such a funny expression and mock heroics. "Oh disaster!" said he. And then he explained that he had been ducked in the fountain as a penalty for being sober! The bombast in his doublet and galligaskins had bonded together in lumps because he was unable to leave the festivities to change until His Majesty retired.

Robert has, once more, shown much greatness in a little frame. So much attention and expenditure ruined and made ridiculous. Yet he remains hospitable.

=== **1610** ===

=== **1590** ===

=== **1560** ===

=== **1560** ===

=== **1580** ===

=== **1610** ===